**Good News
On Sunday Morning:**

**Sermons from
St. Matthew Baptist Church**

By the Reverend Doctor
Louis V Alexander

Good News
on Sunday Morning:

Sermons from
St. Matthew Baptist Church

By the Rev. Louis V. Alexander

ISBN:978-1-936497-15-7

Scripture taken from the
Authorized (King James) Version
(KJV)

St. Matthew Baptist Church
2600 Warren Avenue
Dallas, TX 75215

Manufactured in the United States of America

Dedication

This collection of sermons is dedicated:

To my father and mother:
L.Z. and Lorene Alexander

To my wonderful wife of thirty-six (36) years:
Marlene Alexander

To all six of my children:
Trent, Victor, Torin, Natasha Nicole, Louis Jr. and **Natasha Evonne**

To the greatest church this side of glory:
The St. Matthew Baptist Church
2600 Warren Avenue, Dallas, TX

To great teachers that touched my life:
Reverend C.O. Smith –
Mt. Horeb Baptist Church, Waxahachie, TX

Dr. Norman Robinson –
Mt. Olive Baptist Church, Arlington, TX

Dr. Thomas Payne –
Pearly Gate Baptist Church, Dallas, TX

Dr. Gordon Munford –
Southern Bible Institute (SBI), Dallas, TX

Dr. Mal Couch –
Tyndale Theological Seminary, Ft. Worth, TX

Dr. Charles Reed –
Instructor, SBI, Dallas, TX

David Daniels – High School Principal, Grand Prairie, TX

Reverend McKinley Jackson –
Samaria Baptist Church, Ft. Worth, TX

Reverend Samuel Washington –
New Hope Baptist Church – Kerens, TX

Table of Contents

Justification

Romans 3:24-28

Justification is a word that is of great importance, to every born again believer. This word is just as important as the assurance of salvation (knowing that you are saved). I venture to say that a clear understanding of justification is just as important as eternal security (knowing that once you are saved, you cannot be lost). A clear understanding of justification has much to do with a believer's attitude toward God the Father, God the Son, and God the Holy Spirit, a better attitude will develop a better relationship.

Let's define justification that we might understand what we are discussing; Justification is a divine act whereby an infinitely Holy God judicially declares a believing sinner to be righteous and acceptable before Him, because Christ has borne the sinners sin on the cross, and has been made unto Him righteous. Isn't that wonderful, God justly declares righteous the one who believes on Jesus Christ?

In verse 24, the root meaning of the English word "justified," is to make righteous, or to vindicate, or to exonerate, to be justified is to be acquitted. To be justified means that the sinner's record is wiped clean, never to be brought up again. Make no mistake about it my brothers and sisters; we did not receive probation. We have been justified; probation is a method or time of testing. It is a conditional release of a prisoner or of the guilty. To be justified is far better than probation; we must bear in mind that probation can be revoked. And we also need to be aware of the fact, that to be "justified" is more than a mere pardon, to be pardoned is to be excused, to forgive to free from penalty. It is to be released from punishment. Jesus did all of this for us, but when you are pardoned only, there is a possibility that you can still be guilty of a crime, it's just that you were excused, forgiven.

Again to be "justified" clears the record. Every born again believer is righteous in the eyes of God, your record is clear. God will never bring up what you use to be or what you do and He does not hold those things against you, because they are remembered no more. Romans 5:1 says, "Therefore being justified by faith, we have peace with God through Lord Jesus Christ;" If it be so that we have peace with God, then it is true, that He remembers our sins no more. I said that God does not hold, what we use to be or what we use to do against us, look at Romans 5:9, "Much more then, being now justified by His blood, we shall be saved from wrath."

Notice in Romans 3:24, "justified freely," the Greek word from which "freely" is translated, is related to the word "gift." Theodore H. Epp declares that this word "freely" could be translated "gift." God justified us (sinners that is), yet there was nothing in us that would make God want to justify us. We were unattractive, and unclean. Why would God justify us? Here is the answer: it's all in Jesus Christ. Once a sinner trust Jesus Christ as Savior, God justifies him freely, just as one gives another a gift. I know what you are thinking, if justification is free, it must be cheap, but I beg to differ with you. It was bought with a tremendous price of the blood of Jesus. We cannot calculate that price, we cannot estimate that price. We only know that "Jesus paid it all, and all to Him I owe sin has left a crimson stain, but He washed it white as snow."

Verse 24, again, "Being made righteous before God freely," listen to this verse, "by His grace." "Being made righteous before God freely by His grace." Justified by God's grace, that means that fallen mankind has nothing to do with pronouncing themselves righteous. It is entirely by the grace of God. Let me try to tell you what grace is in a simple way, grace is something that we don't deserve; God just gives it out of the riches of His love. Grace is the unmerited gift of God; grace is that which God wants to give us. We actually deserve punishment, but because of what Jesus has done at Calvary, God justifies the sinner freely when he places his faith in

Jesus Christ. Now there was nothing good in us, read II Corinthians 5:21: "For He hath made Him to be sin for us, who knew no sin; that we might be made the righteousness of God in Him." All that we have is in Jesus Christ; all that we are is in Jesus Christ.

Let me read verse 24 again, "Being made righteous before God freely by His undeserving gift." Listen to the last part of this verse, "through the redemption that is in Christ Jesus." Redemption, that word means a loosing particularly by paying a price, to deliver by paying a price. There are three words that might interest us when we speak of redemption, *agorazo*, *exagorazo*, and *lutroo*. *Agorazo*, means to purchase in the market place, this carries the thought of a slave market. The subjects of redemption are "sold under sin," but even worst they are under a sentence of death, and the purchase price is the redeemer who died in our stead, Galatians 3:13, "Christ has redeemed us from the curse of the law, being made a curse for us: for it is written, Cursed is everyone that hangeth on a tree."

Exagorazo means "to buy out of the market." The redeemed are never to be exposed to sale. *Lutroo*, that means "to loose, to set free by paying a price." I need to read verse 24 once more, "Being made righteous before God freely by His undeserving gift, through paying a price to deliver lost sinners that is in Jesus Christ." I can see mankind, weak, helpless, without strength, no sense of direction, wandering nomads, caught up in darkness, stumbling along the way.

Justification is a word that gives you a feeling of having been on trial. I firmly believe that Paul wants us to feel the divine court room of God. In that divine court room, all of mankind is declared to be guilty. Romans 3:10 says, "There is none righteous no not one." Romans 3:11 says, "There is none that understandeth, there is none that seek after God." Verse 12 goes on to say, "They are all gone out of the way, they are together become unprofitable; there is none that doeth good, no not one."

Here we have just a few charges against mankind as we sit in the court room God; Romans 3:13, "Their throat is an open grave." That means the vilest and most loathsome things can come out of an un-regenerated person's mouth. And that unregenerate person stinks as an open grave.

The second charge is in verse 13, "With their tongues they have used deceit." That means that the unregenerate person takes pleasure in murdering folk with their tongues, always busy tearing someone down. But we need to remember that the mouth will only speak that which is in the heart.

The third charge against mankind is found in verse 14, "Whose mouth is full of cursing and bitterness": The mouth a cesspool of ungodliness, cursing, slandering, and gossip. It does not matter whether the gossip is true or not, just a bad mouth.

Listen to the charges against mankind, as we sit in the courtroom of God, charges five and six, "their feet are swift to shed blood and destruction and misery are in their ways." Paul says in verse 23, "For all have sinned, and come short of the glory of God." Mankind was guilty as charged, guilty on fourteen accounts. God is justifiably angry with sinners. They have rebelled against Him and cut themselves off from His life giving power. They have transgressed, they have over stepped the boundary between right and wrong.

Mankind is guilty, and the penalty is death. But wait; as mankind is leaving God's court room, our lawyer Jesus Christ said something to God the righteous Judge. And the Holy Spirit told Paul to write the words God spoke in that court room, Romans 8:1, "There is therefore now no condemnation to them which are in Christ Jesus, who walk not after the flesh, but after the Spirit."

That means my brothers and sisters, case dismissed. It's all in Jesus Christ, everything we have is in Him; justification, grace, and redemption, and now we can sing with the song writer, "I'm free praise the Lord I'm free no longer bound, no more chains holding me." I was convicted, but not condemned, Jesus took my condemnation out on the cross one Friday evening died, and was raised, early Sunday morning with all power in His hands.

Unger says, "That justification springs from the fountain of God's grace" (Titus 3: 4-5). It is operative as the result of the redemptive and propitiatory sacrifice of Christ, who has settled all the claims of the law (Romans 3:24-25; 5:9).

Systematic theology points out that the believer is constituted righteous by virtue of his position in Christ, but he is justified by a declaratory decree of God. Righteousness imputed is the abiding fact, and justification is the divine recognition of that fact. There is no justification provided for man which is not eternal in character.

Sin

Romans 6:23

The word sin is so complex, that it's almost impossible to define or examine it in forty five minutes, sin last Sunday we said, had been imputed unto us, because of our forefather Adam. Romans 5:12, tell us, "wherefore, as by one man sin entered into the world, and death by sin; an so death passed upon all men, for that all have sinned." The first Adam ruined the human race. Adam sinned, and therefore he was only capable of begetting posterity like himself other sinners. Every human being was in the loins of Adam when he disobeyed God, when Adam sinned we sinned. Adams was the Federal head, when Adam fell, the human race fell.

Then too we talked about sin, there are personal sins, omission and commission, either we have been an active participant in wrong or we have been a none-participant in a direct command of God. Romans 3:23 says, "For all have sinned and come short of the glory of God." What this passage of scripture is really saying is "for all have sinned and are continuously coming short of the glory of God.

Again when we speak of sin, we must never forget our sin nature, every child of Adam is born with the Adamic nature, and that nature is never eradicated in this life. Listen! Men do not sin and become sinners, men sin because they have a sin nature. Now those born again believers, those who have accepted Christ as their Personal Savior, and those who have been indwelled by the Holy Spirit, they have some overcoming power. In Galatians 5:11, they are summon to, "walk in the Spirit." The born again believer ought to be spirit led, Spirit controlled. Notice I said ought to be, that's not the case all the time. I John 4:4 say, "Greater is he that is in you, than he that is in the world."

For the wages of sin is death: but the gift of God eternal life." The ultimate pay for sin is death; those who continue in sin should expect death. I think that we should look at death in two ways this morning: spiritual death and physical death. Now if I'm reading the scripture correctly, "the wages of sin is death." That means that my mother gave birth to a boy child that was spiritually dead.

The 51st division of Psalms, verse 5 says, "Behold, I was shapen in iniquity; and in sin did my mother conceive me." It has to be true if the wages of sin is death." And I'm Adam's descendant, and Adam's sin was imputed unto me, then I was spiritually dead. I know you are wondering, what does it mean to be spiritually dead? To be spiritually dead is to not possess the Spirit of God. Ephesians 2:1 teaches that truth, that a sinner is dead in trespasses and sin; verse five repeats that same principle.

So if my mother (Lorene) gave birth to a spiritual dead boy, then what Jesus said to Nicodemus is absolutely necessary "you must be born again. "Except a man be born of water and of the Spirit, he cannot enter into the kingdom of God." But it is the second birth that places us in the family of God it is a spiritual transformation. The water and the Spirit is that resurrection power that raises the spiritually dead to a new life. II Corinthians 5:17, "Therefore if any man be in Christ, he is a new creature: old things are passed away; behold all things are new." A better translation is "new creation."

"For the wages of sin is death." Not only did my mother give birth to a boy child that was spiritually dead, but she gave birth to a boy that started dying physically the moment, he was born. I hasten to mention Adam's sin was reckoned on my behalf, so the truth of the matter is, like Adam, I die a little daily. The moment my mother gave birth to me, death got on my trail, the moment you were born death zeroed in on you, oh, yes, he might wear different hats: high blood pressure, blocked arteries, abnormal heart beat, cancer, kidney failure, strokes.

There has been a step between you and death

from day one. What an awful predicament it is that mankind has been press into death and man is bound to meet. Hebrews 9:27, tells us, "And as it is appointed unto men once to die, but after this judgment." Death has always had one eye on me and you.

Enoch walked with God so close that death couldn't touch him; Elijah caught a whirlwind and did not see death. Listen there are little signs along the way that we that warn you of deaths progress the grey hair is a sign, that he is closing in on you, glasses to read with is a sign that death is closing in on you. No back-teeth to chew with are a sign that death is closer today than he was yesterday. Hebrews 9:27 tell us, "And as it is appointed into men once to die, but after this judgment." Physical death is the consequence of sin. "For the wages of sin is death."

Let's try and understand this word wages in the Greek there are two words for wages: *misthos* and *opsonion*. *Misthos* has to do with receiving wages from being hired, or it has to do with reward, this is not the word that's used in our scripture text. *Opsonion* is the word that used here in Romans 6:23, it is a soldier's rations, now Roman soldiers lived from the loot taken in war, and they sold their prisoners to the slave merchants who follow the armies to battle. They lived on rations, *opsonion*, so far the rations of sin is death, it is not paid in a lump sum, but it is measured out day by day. Death is sin's due reward, and it must be paid. A master employ's a man, and it is due to that man that he should receive his wages. Now, if sin did not entail death and misery, it would be an injustice. Sin, must be punished, they that sow must reap. The sin, which hires you, must pay.

I know what you are thinking here, is there a way out, and is there any hope for mankind? Should we look for a hero? Let's read again, "For the wages of sin is death. But the gift of God is eternal life through Jesus Christ our Lord." The gift of God. Free gifts, charisma, Barnhouse calls this free gift a grace gift. In the Greek language, there is not much difference between, grace (*Charis*) and free gift (*Charisma*). God has a gift; as a matter of fact it's a free gift that he wants to give. God want to give eternal like, II Peter 2:9 says, "He's not willing that any should perish, but that all should come to repentance."

This free gift is offered to all Jews and Gentiles, the rich and the poor, the learned and the unlearned. I know the free gift is an offer, I hear Him saying come now, let us reason together, saith the Lord: though your sins be as scarlet, they shall be as white as snow: "Though they be like crimson they shall be as wool." The free gift is offered, "For whosoever shall call upon the name of the Lord shall be saved."

The free gift is offered to all, but we must bear in mind, it's through Jesus Christ our Lord." Sin and death came by Adam, now righteousness, and eternal life came by Jesus Christ, we had no righteousness of our own, we were depraved, we were lost, we were far from God. The righteousness of God is imputed to those who believe. According to Romans 3:19 and 20, Abraham believed the promise of God and verse 22 says it was imputed unto us. If we believe in him that raised Jesus our Lord from the dead, and we have nothing to do with our righteousness. It's in Jesus Christ. Jesus became the sin bearer, He identified with us in the flesh. He became one of us that we might be made righteous in Him.

Isaiah 53:5, "But he was wounded for our transgressions, He was bruised for our iniquities: the chastisement of our peace was upon Him; and with His stripes we are healed."

John 1:36, says, "Behold the Lamb of God." At Calvary, Jesus became my substitute, He died in my place. At Calvary, He took my sins upon Him,

"*Eli, Eli lama sabachthani.* (My God, my God, why has thou forsaken me?)"

At Calvary, His blood washed away all my sins, the blood that makes me whiter than snow. If you want to live forever, you must come by Calvary. God gave Him to us at Bethlehem, but he gave Him for us at Calvary. Leave Calvary and come to the empty tomb. We serve a risen Savior.

Getting Past the
Constant Struggle of Life

Romans 7:15

I watched my niece (Courtney) Wednesday night moving around in the middle aisle. She was only eleven months old. As I watched her, she would take six or seven steps and fall. She would sit for a few moments, and she would then get up and take off again. Courtney would take five or six more steps, stagger, take two more steps, and then fall. While watching her, I discovered that we have Christians constantly struggling just like that baby. I watched Courtney, and I said to myself that in time she has to get pass the falling every few steps.

I come by to tell you this morning that I believe a Christian can get pass the constant struggle. The baby Courtney really wants to go ahead and walk. They have the desire, but they just can't pull it off. I believe there are Christians that want to go ahead and live for Jesus, but they just can't pull it off.

Notice verse fifteen: "For that which I do I allow not, for what I would, that do I not: but what I hate, that do I." As struggling Christians we think, I'm always doing what I don't want to do. I know what I want to do, but I can't do it. I'm always doing that I hate. What is wrong with me? It seems as though something is out of control. There is an attraction or a magnetic force in me that moves me to do the very things I hate. I'm a Christian, and I truly love the Lord. He is my Savior. What's the matter with me? It's as though I'm sick or hooked on something. I don't know what I'm doing. What I want to do, I don't do; however, what I hate I do.

My behavior baffles me. I'm always falling when I ought to be walking. I'm struggling when I ought to be free. I know I heard the preacher say that II Corinthians declares, "Therefore if any man be in Christ, he is a new creature. Old things are passed away; behold all things are become new." I know there has been a change in my life, but I'm still doing what I hate. I don't want to be like this, I'm torn between right and wrong or good and bad.

Once we are converted, we have two natures: the old nature and the new nature. The old nature is of Adam, and the new nature is of the Spirit. The old nature links us to all that sin is, and the new nature links to all that is righteousness is. Off times these two can cause us problems in our daily walk. The old nature and the new nature never agree they are always at odds. If the new nature says drink Kool-Aid, and the old nature will say it has no bite and it's a drink for kids. It will say drink Coors. The new nature says that it's wrong to drink Coors and call yourself Holy. The old nature will reply who's going to tell, and just one can't hurt. You are in the middle. The old nature is pulling to the left, and the new nature is pulling to the right. If you drink the Coors you feel as if, "What I hate that do I." It is your vote that carries the motion. Every Christian has a choice to make, Romans 6:12,13 says, "Let not sin therefore reign in your mortal body, that ye should obey it in the lust thereof, neither yield ye your members as instruments of unrighteousness unto sin: but yield yourselves unto God."

There is a hint of personal responsibility in Romans 6:12 your and ye referring to the new you. The control of the Christian's body is in the Christian's hands. He has the will. If there is a constant struggle in your life, it's your fault. The choice is yours.

Notice verses 16 and 17, "If then, I do that which I would not, I consent unto the law that it is good. Now then it is no more I that do it but sin that dwelleth in me." There was nothing wrong with the law because it was Holy, but the problem was with Paul. He was trying to live his new life under the law. However, the law could not produce holiness in Paul's life. Not because the law was weak, but because the flesh is weak. In Romans 7:14, Paul says that the law is spiritual, but I am carnal sold under sin. The carnal Christian allows the sin nature to control him after he's saved, even though he does not have to let the sin nature (the old nature) do so. Those who have not experientially found deliverance from the power of sin are carnal Christians. Those who are constantly struggling are carnal Christians. There's going to be some struggle, but not a continual struggle.

Listen to verse seventeen, "Now then it is no more I that do it, but sin that dwelleth in me." Sin here in this verse represents, the nature (the old nature), which is different from sins. Sins are manifestations or expressions of the old nature. Let's read verse seventeen again, "Now then it is no more I that do it, but sin (the old nature) that dwelleth in me." It's what I received from Adam, it is bad blood, that makes bad nature, and bad nature is known by the fruit it produces: illegitimate children, homosexual, prostitution of women and children. Bad nature is known by the fruit it produces: pornography, lesbianism, drugs, murder, greed, hate, anger, no thought of God.

Verse 18 says, "For I know that in me (that is in my flesh) dwelleth no good thing: for to will is present with me: but how to perform that which is good I find not." I'm helpless. My old nature, the flesh, isn't any good. My new nature that the spirit implanted when I was born again wants to do good, but I don't know how to execute that which is good. I'm helpless. There is disorder in me, and it frustrates the purpose for which God saved me. He told me and all believers, "Ye are the light of the world." I can't shine, when the old keeps defeating the new, when the old keeps leading me in an unholy path. I'm helpless! I'm defeated, verse nineteen, "For the good that I would I do not: but the evil which I would not, that I do." I have got a problem. I'm a Christian, but I'm still doing evil. There's no joy in what I'm doing, yet I can't restrain myself. Verse twenty is almost a repeat of verse seventeen.

Let me summarize verses 21, 22, and 23. The law of sin in my members fights against the law of my mind and brings me into captivity to the law of my old nature which is in my members. I love the law of my God. My mind knows and understands God's law. However, I am defeated. I can't do what I know is right.

Let me close here with verse 24: "O wretched man that I am! Who shall deliver me from the body of this death?" This is the cry of the defeated who really wanted to live Holy, but he couldn't. This is the cry of the helpless, who really wanted to be a helper. This is the cry of a carnal Christian who has not founded deliverance from the power of sin. "O wretched man that I am." This is a cry of despair; notice the exclamation mark at the end of the sentence. "Who shall deliver me from the body of this death?"

Let me try to brand this verse in your mind. Picture if you would a man wandering around in the wilderness, and there is a dead man tied to his back. They are tied back to back. Their arms and wrists are tied together. Where ever the living man goes, so goes the dead man. After a few days, the dead man starts to rot and stink. Soon the rotten, stinking dead man starts to infect the live man. Everywhere the live man goes there's stink and corruption. That dead man is sin, and he sure will corrupt you and cause you to stink.

As I close this morning, if you are struggling don't give up. There is hope for the hopeless. There is strength for the weak. There is control for the wavering, and there is joy for the wretched. "Who shall deliver me from the body of this death?" Here is the answer in the 25th verse, "I thank God through Jesus Christ our Lord." It's in Jesus, deliverance is in Jesus. In Chapter 8 and verse 2, I got something new in my life. "For the law of the Spirit of life in Christ Jesus hath made me free from the law of sin and death." I'm free! I'm free! From sin and death, at

Calvary, Jesus broke death's hold. At Calvary, sin nature (old nature) was judged and dethroned. Jesus left word through Paul, I'm dead to sin. I'm walking in the Spirit.

Paul's Masterpiece

Romans 1:1-2

This letter was written from Corinth during Paul's third visit to that city. C.I. Scofield dates this letter in A.D. 60, but Irving L. Jensen says it was written in A.D. 56. When Paul wrote this letter Rome was the largest and most important city in the world (estimated population: one to four millions). The Emperor Nero has just begun to rule (A.D. 54-68), and anti-Christian persecution had not yet begun.

Romans is Paul's masterpiece, a key that unlocks the door to vast treasures of scripture. Scofield says the theme of Romans is, "The Gospel of God." Jensen writes the theme is, "God's salvation for sinners." Theodore H. Epp wrote that the book of Romans was chiefly responsible for the reformation, for it was this book that caused Martin Luther to realize as never before that justification is by faith in Christ alone, not through an institutional church or by works of any kind.

Verse 1, "Paul, a servant of Jesus Christ who was called to be an apostle, separated unto the gospel of God." Paul was his Gentile name, and Saul was his Hebrew name. He became Paul after his conversion, the name Paul means "little after he trusted Jesus Christ as his personal Savior." He was certainly little in his own eyes. I think this should speak to Christians who seek fame and exaltation. When

Christ comes into our lives and we look back at our old ways, certainly we feel little.

Paul referred to himself as "a servant of Jesus Christ." That word servant is also translated "bondman." In the original language, it is pronounced *doulos*, which means "slave." Paul was a willing "slave" of Jesus Christ. A "slave" or a "servant" follows instruction he makes no decision on his own. He simply does what his master tells him to do. He does not stand around saying I'm grown, or I do what I want to do.

A slave takes orders and goes where he's told and does what he is instructed to do. There are not many servants around anymore. We got some church goers, but not many servants. Most folk these days want to be served. Before Paul trusted Jesus Christ as his personal Savior, he was a slave to sin. He did exactly what he felt like doing, his sin nature, and the society he lived in had him bounded, they dictated his life style: Football game on Sunday, water skiing on Sunday, picnic in the park on Sunday, concert on Saturday night, Poker on Saturday. After he came to Jesus, Paul realized that he had been bought with a price. He wrote in I Corinthians 6:19, 20, "What? Know ye not that your body is the temple of the Holy Ghost which is in you, which ye have of God. And ye are not your own? For ye are bought with a price: Therefore glorify God in your body, And in your spirit which are God's."

Loosed from Satan and bound to Jesus, but he is a willing slave. I wish I had time to talk about the benefits of being bound to Jesus Christ; like translated into the kingdom, being a citizen of Heaven, being the sons and daughters of the most High God. But I don't have the time.

Verse 1, "Paul, a servant of Jesus Christ and a willing slave of Jesus Christ, was called to be an apostle." He was "called to be an apostle," Paul never forgot his vocation; he was an official representative of Jesus Christ. He had been called to a position, and he never forgot his calling. Where ever he stood, he was standing there for Jesus. When he spoke, he was speaking for Jesus. Whatever Paul was doing, he was doing it for Jesus, and his life was about Jesus. No more I, but Christ. Being a "slave" and an apostle seem to have something in common.

What we needed today are some representatives. I discovered that we don't need more singers in the church. We don't even need better singers in the church. We don't need a bunch of people with degrees. We don't even need a better dressed people in the church.

We need more representatives, we need people that can say look at me and see Christ in me. I'm living for and I'm working for Jesus. "Called to be an apostle," Jesus Christ is the one who does the calling. Not your grandmother who decided you look like a preacher, or a friend who told you that you sound like a preacher. No dreams in the night and you woke up in a cold sweat.

I want to be clear right here. Jesus does the calling. Jesus said in John 15:16, "Ye have not chosen me, but I have chosen you, and ordained you, that ye should go and bring forth fruit, and that your fruit should remain: that whatsoever ye shall ask of my father in my name. He may give it to you."

"Called to be an apostle," *Apostolos* is the correct pronunciation in the original language, it means, one sent with a message. Not one that went on his own, but one sent with a message. Wait, I can prove it. Look at the last portion of verse 1, "separated unto the gospel of God." That word separated. Paul gives a description of himself "separated" simply means "set apart." Paul knew what the will of God was for his life, and he was set apart to accomplish that will. Every born again believer ought to know what God's will is for his or her life. We are not saved just to be saved, but we ought to be busy populating the kingdom. Each of us has been called to a work (a ministry).

Ephesians 4:11-12, "And He gave some apostles; and some, prophets, and some evangelists; and some, pastors and teachers." "For the perfecting of the saints, for the work of the ministry, for the edifying of the body of Christ." But you can't do anything until the Lord gives the orders. We got some folk doing, yet they have not been told what to do. It's a mess when you are busy and you don't know what God's will is for your life. You are an evangelist without a message. Know what God's will is for your life. Listen, the only way we can populate the kingdom is to tell men about Jesus Christ, and I know that fits in God's will.

Verse 1, "Separated unto the gospel of God" "Set apart" "Unto the gospel of God." Not just "set apart" to look good, just look like a Christian. "Come here; look at me with my long dress on. My hair is natural. I wear no makeup. See my big bible. Speak to me so that I can tell you I'm blessed of the Lord." Not set apart for church on Sunday. Paul says, "Set apart unto the gospel of God." I know somebody is asking, "What is the gospel of God?" I am glad you asked. It's not a soft drink that we can share after church. It's not some auxiliary in the church. The gospel of God is about Jesus Christ, His death, burial, and resurrection. That's what sinners need to hear. They need to hear about Jesus.

In Matthew 28: 19, Jesus says, "All power is given unto me in heaven and in earth. Go ye therefore, and teach all nations, baptizing them in the name of the father, and the son, and of the Holy Ghost. Teaching them to observe all things whatsoever I have commanded you: And lo, I am with you always, even unto the end of the world. Amen. Jesus says, "Tell them!"

"Paul, a willing slave of Jesus Christ called to be sent with a message, set apart unto the good news from God concerning His son Jesus Christ." Verse 2: "which he had promised afore by His prophets in the Holy Scriptures." Paul says my message is not something new, it was promised before, and is now being openly made known.

Isaiah talked about Jesus Christ 600 years before he came. In the 53rd chapter Isaiah says, "He is despised and rejected of men; a man of sorrows, and acquainted with grief: and we hid as it were our faces from Him; He was despised, and we esteemed

Him not. Surely He hath borne our griefs, and carried our sorrows: yet we did esteem him stricken, smitten of God, and afflicted. But He was wounded for our transgression, He was bruised for our iniquities: the chastisement of our peace was upon Him; and with his stripes we are healed."

That's Jesus, y'all. "All we like sheep have gone astray, we turned everyone to his own way and the Lord hath laid on Him the iniquity of us all." This is my verse. "He was oppressed, and He was afflicted, yet He opened not his mouth: He is brought as a lamb to the slaughter and as a sheep before her shearers is dumb, so He openeth not His mouth."

The old preacher said, "He never said a mumbling word". Paul said in verse 15, "I am ready to preach the gospel to you that Rome also." I'm ready to preach, His redemption. How he redeemed us. He paid it all, and all to Him I owe. We were sold under sin, but His blood that flows from Calvary paid the price. I am ready to preach. I'm ready to preach justification. The case against us has been dismissed. I'm ready to preach propitiation. I'm ready to preach sanctification. I'm ready to preach glorification. In verse 3, Paul says, "He is Lord." Wherever there is a servant, there must be a master, Lord Kurios.

Grace Beyond Logic

Romans 8: 28

There is no logic in this passage of scripture. These words left logic stranded on a hill somewhere trying to reason over what has been said. Logic says two plus two is four, but this passage of scripture says to me that two plus two can very well be six. Then it says to me, "Don't try to understand it, just believe it when God is involved. God works beyond the circle of logic, two plus two equals six when God is in your life, and when you are in the will of God. With God comes the extra-ordinary, such as never been seen, heard or done before. God is amazing. He's astonishing. He is a wonder. He's a figure that we can't figure out. That's why two plus two can equal six when God is in your life.

Logic does not interfere with God's doing. When God is at work, logic must be dismissed. Maybe there is someone here that doesn't know what logic does. Logic sits down and reasons, calculates, and thinks and thinks. Then logic says, "It's possible. It will work. It can be done." Logic deals with the probability of the matter. Logic says, "It is impossible. It will never work." Logic says, "If you walk through the Red Sea, you are sure to get soaking wet, and there is an eighty percent chance you might drown. But God takes a whole nation, and march them through the Red Sea, they went in dry and they came out dry. Oh yes! God did not lose a soul. You cannot approach God with logic, and certainly you cannot live for God and deal in logic. That's the problem with the modern day Christians, they want a logical God, a God that they can understand and predict.

Faith is the avenue to God and it is the means by which we walk with Him daily. We are summons to believe God without always understanding Him. Can you believe our scripture text this morning? "And we know that a-l-l things work together for good to them that love God, to them who are the called according to his purpose." Now I don't understand divine chemistry, how God can take "All things," and transform them into good. I don't understand it but I believe it, I don't understand how He can compute disaster into good.

I want to talk about four things briefly:
1. God's affection
2. God's expectation
3. God's purpose
4. And all things working together for the good.

I. This passage of scripture segregates; notice the words we and them, those words suggest that there is a group set apart from others, a group that God is involved with. In this passage of scripture, we and them are those who have accepted Jesus as their personal Savior. We and them points out those who are standing on the promises of God, those who are recipient of the benefits that only God can give. This scripture is not speaking to any and everybody, only to those who have believed the report; and the report is that Jesus is the Christ son of the Living God. He died for our sins and was raised for our Justification. We and them are the ones standing on the promise of eternal life. Jesus said in St. John 10:28, "And I give unto them eternal life; and they shall never perish, neither shall any man pluck them out of my hand."

There's that man word "them" again. It's segregation. Believers are separated from non-believers. The new believers are sinners, the believers are saints. Sinners are to be judged and are to endure eternal damnation in hell, while believers are to enjoy eternal bliss with the Lord. Though the Bible segregates, yet it does not fail to invite others to become one of them (A believer).

In Matthew 11:28, Jesus says come unto me, all ye that labour and are heavy laden and I will give you rest." That's an invitation. Mark 10:21, "Come take up the cross, and follow me," an invitation. Isaiah 1:18, come now, and let us reason together."

And the Bible also gives instruction on how to become one of them. Romans 10:9, "That if thou shalt confess with thy mouth the Lord Jesus and shalt believe in thine heart that God hath raised him from the dead, thou shall be saved. Romans 10:13, "For whosoever shall call upon the name of the Lord shall be saved."

Those two verses are the best instruction I know for becoming one of them. Wouldn't you like to be one of them (a Christian that is) so that God can be working all things together for the good on your behalf? It's up to you to desegregate, and the only way to do that is to come to Jesus. You can't buy your way into this you can't even shoot your way into this. You got to come to Jesus.

II. Secondly, I want to talk about God's expectation; Look at our scripture again, "And we know." I believe that there are some things; God wants his children to know. I am certain that he wants us to know that he is Our Father. In Luke 11:2 Jesus said to his disciples, "When ye pray, say Our Father which art in Heaven."

We should listen closer to the words of Jesus; there are many things He wants us to know. In St. Matthew 6: 25-34, Jesus teaches us not to worry concerning food and drink for the body. Don't worry concerning clothing for the body. In essence, he says your Heavenly Father will take care of you. Jesus expects you to know that God is looking out for you. Singing "He cares for you" is alright. But when you-really-know-down-in-your-heart that God cares for me, you don't have to worry. You can say with the psalmist, "In thee, O Lord, do I put my trust; let me never be ashamed."

Paul said in Philippians 4:19, "But my God shall supply all of your need according to His riches in glory by Christ Jesus." God expects you to know. I think I need to tell you also that God expect you to love Him. Listen to the scripture, "And we know that all things work together for good to them that love God."

God the Creator, our Father has feelings. Let me try to prove it, Genesis 6:6, teaches that it grieved God's heart that he made man upon the earth, Hebrew 3:10, teaches that God was grieved with Israel for forty years because of their unbelief. God has feeling, he grieves over us, and there are times He delights in us.

Have you bowed lately or just paused and said to Him, "God, I love you?" Now after you tell God, you love Him, here's how you express that love. St. John 14:15 says: "If ye love me keep my commandment."

You can't run around here living low-down and say you love God. God says loving me is to do as I say. Nothing is going to work together for the good unless you love God. It's loving God that converts life's pitfalls into good. It's loving God that transforms our worst nightmares into joys. Listen! We have something to do. We couldn't leave it all up to God. Mark 12:30 says, "And thou shalt love the Lord thy God with all thy heart, and with all thy soul, and with all thy mind, and with all thy strength: this is the first commandment."

III. Thirdly, I would like to talk about God's purpose; it's in our scripture, let's read it one more time. "And we know that all things work together for the good to them that love God, to them who are called according to His purpose."

Our whole lives were outlined according to God's plan; he knew just what each one of us would do. God always sees the end as well as the beginning. To get the full purpose, we must look quickly at verse 29, "for whom He did foreknow, He also did predestinate to be conform to the image of His son, that He might be the firstborn among many brethren."

Don't let that word predestinate throw you. It shows that God has set His heart on doing something for us. His purpose has a goal in view, and God is going to see that you reach that goal. Verse 29, tells us what God has in mind. Listen! That we "be conformed to the image of his Son."

God wants us to inwardly share the likeness of his Son, so He predestined, or foreordained us to be like Christ Jesus. God not only knows the goal He has in mind for each of us. He also knows what it will take to make us like Jesus, and He works in us to make us just like Him.

(A) Sometime God's work in us and on us is painful, but God knows what it will take to make us just like Jesus. Philippians 1:6 talks about God working in the believer and that He will keep on working in us and on us until Jesus come. God's work in us and on us is painful sometimes. God's work in us and on us is misunderstood sometimes and even Satan tries to disguise his work as God's work sometime, but the text says, "All things work together for the good to them that love God, to them who are called according to His purpose."

It does not matter who's doing it, God is the power that's going to work it out for the good, for me and you. God is in control of the all things.

(B) If it seems like sometime you can hardly pay your rent, and every time it looks like you might get ahead, something will happen to set you back, don't worry – it's going to work out for good. Don't worry about the mountains you have to climb, it's for the good. If you have been sick and it looks like you can't get well, all sickness is not unto death. God is going to work it out for the good.

If your home seems like a battlefield, and it seems like you are the only one leaning on His everlasting arms, just remember that "All thing work together for the good to them that love God." Painful sometimes. God's work in us and on us sometimes is needed to build a closer relationship with Him, and oh how rich you can be spiritually when you live close to God. Don't jump overboard; you might be just what that home needs.

1. Don't worry about stormy days, it's for the good.
2. Don't worry about you midnights; God is in the shadow it's for the good. "Weeping might endure for a night, but joy cometh in the morning."

I might not have money but He's working on me when my house note is past due. He's working on me but I know it's for the good.

Whosoever That Call

Romans 10:13

I. A great surge of joy rose in my heart when I read this passage of scripture. So I read it over and over again. I wanted to cling to every word that Paul spoke, and as these words fell upon my heart, I realized that these words have been a lifeline for many drowning souls. These words have been with mankind throughout the ages to save those who were sinking to rise no more.

Paul was not the first to paint these words upon the pages of this Holy Book, in the book of Joel Chapter 2 verse 32. The prophet Joel says, "And it shall come to pass, that whosoever shall call on the name of the Lord shall be delivered."

I don't know about you, but some 14 years ago I needed those words, "For whosoever shall call upon the name of the Lord shall be saved." There might be someone here this morning in need of a lifeline just let me share this scarlet cord with you.

(A) The first thing that I noticed about this passage is that it is instantaneous. That means that a sinner can be saved without delay, immediately just as soon as he says, "Lord, save me. Come into my life. I'm a sinner. Save me."

As soon as the words are spoken, the Lord will

honor that call. It does not say whosoever shall call upon the name of the Lord shall be saved tomorrow. This scripture does not command us to tarry at a certain place. In a flash, a dirty low down sinner can become a saint, just by calling upon the name of the Lord. You don't have to mix this with three cups of water and wait thirty minutes.

This demands some faith, not great faith, just some faith. It's not quantity that's the issue here, but quality. It's not how much faith one has, but it's the pureness, the richness of one's faith. Now verse seventeen of chapter ten, tells us, "faith cometh by hearing, and hearing by the word of God."

So before a sinner can be instantaneously lifted from a state of being lost, he must hear the word of God, Faith in Jesus Christ is produced by the word of God. So there is no delay, if you are a sinner, you can be saved right now.

II. "For whosoever shall call upon the name of the Lord shall be saved." Another thought, that the Holy Spirit gave birth to as I read this passage over and over again is its simplicity. There is nothing complex in this scripture; it does not have two or more related parts. This is just a simple scripture that anyone can understand.

Look at this scripture closely, it's not a paradox. There is nothing in these words that seems contradictory, or unbelieving, but yet may be true in fact. But this is plain, "whosoever shall call upon the name of the Lord shall be saved."

There is nothing with in the contents of this passage that's mind boggling. It is man that made the way of salvation complicated. Some folks are guilty of trying to recreate the day of Pentecost. They will ask you if you have spoken in tongue. Speaking in tongue is not a prerequisite for salvation, nor is it a part of God's plan of salvation. Paul said in Ephesians 2:8, "For by grace are ye saved through faith; and that not of yourselves; it is the gift of God."

Here we have an explanation of salvation. Though it is incomplete when it is removed from this chapter, nevertheless it is an explanation. In Romans 10:9, we have the direction of salvation: "That if thou shalt confess with thy mouth the Lord Jesus, and shalt believe in thine heart that God hath raised him from the dead, thou shalt be saved."

That's directions. That's how you become saved. Now Romans 10:13 is just an extension of or an addition of that direction. "For whosoever shall call upon the name of the Lord shall be saved."

It's simple, so simple. Great minds are stumbling over this scripture. I can't understand why everybody wants to do something to get saved. If it's by grace, it's free. If I am to call in a believing manner, it's free. Listen. Don't try to stop drinking, lying, running women, just call and the Lord will do the rest.

III. I read this verse over and over again; I didn't want to miss anything. I wanted to make sure I gave it my best, and when I had done all that my little mind could do by aid of the Holy Spirit. I picked a word from our scripture, and I worked with that word.

I took whosoever from our lesson, this word expresses emphasis on what is being said, this word is to be felt. It is designed to touch those who hear this scripture. Whosoever, this word gives power to what is said, but yet it is tender.

This is like closing your finger in the car door, and you say, 'Oh my finger,' that don't say much. But if you say 'O-h! My finger,' emphasis is put on the word oh and that word is felt by everyone around you and the oh gave power to what was being said.

A. "For whosoever shall call upon the name of the Lord shall be saved." I couldn't turn that word a loose. I looked at it upside down, and I looked at it from the right side and from the left side. I discovered that "whosoever" is a wide word. This word is so wide, that it takes every man, woman, boy and girl within its circle. "Whosoever" means the black and the yellow man. "For whosoever shall call upon the name of the Lord shall be saved. "Whosoever means the rich man and the poor and beggar man. "Whosoever" means the learned and the unlearned man. "Whosoever" includes me and you.

If I had turned to Romans 10:13, and it said if L.V. Alexander shall call upon the name of the Lord, he shall be saved; fear would have gripped my heart. There just might be another L.V. Alexander. Then I couldn't be sure this passage was speaking to me. But when the word said whosoever, I know I'm in that circle.

If a dying man call upon the name of the Lord, he shall be saved. If a drunk, a prostitute call upon the name of the Lord, they shall be saved. If a homosexual calls upon the name of the Lord, he shall be saved. If a lesbian calls upon the name of the Lord, she shall be saved. What a wide word the Lord has given, it's so wide that it leaves no one out. Whosoever is a word that removes all obstruction out of the way, that sinners may lay hold on eternal life.

B. "Whosoever", I have heard that word before, Jesus spoke that wide before, Jesus spoke that wide word in St. John 3:16 "For God so loved the world, that He gave His only begotten Son, that whosoever believeth in Him should not perish, but have everlasting life." The master spoke that word again to the Samaritan woman at Jacob's well, in St. John 4:14." But whosoever drinketh of the water that I shall give him shall never thirst." On another occasion, Jesus said in St. Mark 8:34, "whosoever will come after me, let him deny himself, and take up his cross, and follow me." Listen I'm glad to be one of them, I'm not ashamed to be called a Christian.

C. Our text is an easy text: "For whosoever shall call upon the name of the Lord shall be saved." Anybody can call upon His name, and everybody knows what it is to call, the baby calls from the cradle, although the language be strange, but mother understands. Everybody knows what it is to call. Blind Bartimaeus knew what it was to call. He heard that Jesus was passing by, he called out "Jesus, thou son of David, have mercy on me". When a man calls in a believing way, he shall be saved.

IV. As I close, you might need something to inspire your confidence. You know I purchased a set of tires a few years ago, and there was little sticker on the side that said this tire carries a 20,000 miles warranty. Well there is a guarantee in this scripture, "whosoever shall call upon the name the Lord shall be saved."

The confidence is in the "shall be saved." There are no ifs and no maybe. There is no guessing about it. This is firm. This is fixed. It's unchangeable. God has promised, and He is able to keep His promise to every sinner that call upon His name.

A few years ago, I took the whosoever, and I called on the name of Jesus, I stood on the assurance of shall be, and right now, I know I'm saved. Somebody said, "Alexander how do you know? They wanted me to say I looked new. I looked at my hand, and my hand looked new. I looked at my feet and they did too. That sounds good, but that don't prove anything!

I know I'm saved. Mark 16:16 says, "He that believeth and is baptized shall be saved." I believe on Jesus and I have been baptized, I know I'm saved. Colossians 1:14 tells me, "In whom we have redemption through His blood, even the forgiveness of sins," that means my sins are forgiven.

St. John 1:12 says, "But as many as received Him, to them gave He power to become the sons of

God, even to them that believe on His name." That means I became a child of God.

St. John 5:24, "Verily, verily I say unto you He that heareth my word, and believeth on Him that sent me, hath everlasting life, and shall not come into condemnation but is passed from death unto life."

II Corinthians 5:17 tells us, "therefore if any man be Christ, he is a new creature: old things are passed away: behold all things are become new. I got a new me, I got a new life. It's an inward change that's outwardly expressed. My hands don't look new, they just do new things, and my feet don't look new they just go to new places. My mind is new, and my heart is new.

Acts 4:12, "Neither is there salvation in any other: for there is none other name under heaven given among men, Whereby we must be saved." In case you are shopping around He's the only way. You can't get this at J.C. Penny, you can't get this Sears and Wal-Mart. Jesus is the only way.

He changed me. I've been born again, I can't explain it. It's a mystery how a drunk can be transformed into a preacher. It's a mystery how a prostitute can become a missionary. It's a mystery how a killer can come to sing, "I love the Lord, He hear my cry and pitied every groan. Long as I live and trouble rise, I'll haste unto his throne".

If you want a new mind, call on the Lord. If you want a new heart, call on the Lord. Let Him work on you. He'll fix you. A few years ago, I called and the Lord saved me. It must be the transforming power of the blood from Calvary, the blood that flows from Calvary. "There is a fountain filled with blood, drawn from Emmanuel's veins, sinners plunge beneath the flood lose all their guilty stain".

That they might be saved

Romans 10:

I. Paul cries out for the salvation of his people, one of his desires is to see his people saved. He prays to God for the salvation of Israel. Paul has a special love for his people; he has a love so strong that he is constantly praying for their salvation. Since you are save, who are you constantly praying for where there is a life there is always hope. Sinners don't get too bad for God; they don't get too dirty for Him. The truth of the matter is that sinners need to be saved. The saved ought to be concerned about the unsaved. Every Christian should have an urge to evangelize.

A. Paul is praying for the nation, Israel as a whole, but this people had a few problems. One of those problems Paul points out in verse 2, "For I bear them record that they have a zeal of God, but not according to knowledge."

They had a powerful zeal that was not channeled, no course no directions; they had an passionate eagerness for the cause of righteousness. "They had a zeal for God." Listen! Their zeal might have been as sincere as Abraham's faith, but misdirected zeal is a waste. The nation, Israel, had knowledge of God, but they sought Him in an external way by rule and rites (acts of worship). They missed him. They work hard, they dotted every "I" and they crossed every "T", but they missed Him. They became zealous for the letter and the form instead of for God Himself. We have lots of zealous folk today just working away, Paul made it plain, it's not by works. Paul made it clear in Ephesians 2:8, "For by grace are ye saved through faith. That's not of yourselves. It is the gift of God.

II. Verse 3, "For they being ignorant of God's righteousness, and going about to establish their own righteousness have not submitted themselves unto the righteousness of God."

They did not understand the God kind of righteousness by faith. They misconceived it. They wanted to do something. They wanted to keep the law or work under the law to produce a character that could be approved by God. The law only provides knowledge on sin, but it does not provide salvation for anyone. God's verdict is in Romans 3:23, "All have sinned, and come short of the glory of God."

The Jews were taking pride in the way they kept the law, and they saw no need of trusting Jesus Christ by faith in order to receive righteousness of God. Paul was grieved about this, there are people today that are religious, yet they see no need to trust Jesus Christ. Religion without Jesus is empty, coming to church religiously without knowing Jesus is empty.

The emptiness is not in the church, it's in watching the do's and don'ts. Jesus told Nicodemus, "You must be born again."

Listen, the last portion of verse 3, they "have not submitted themselves unto the righteousness of God."

They have not put themselves under orders to obey. The righteousness of God is not complicated the righteousness of God is Christ himself. He met, in our behalf, every demand of the perfect law of God. I. Corinthians 1:30 teaches that Christ is made unto us wisdom and righteousness, and sanctification and redemption. All of this is a singularly full statement of the whole results of the work of Christ." So Christ is our righteousness, not what we can do or what we have done. Not what your father or mother has done. Not being a member of the Baptist church or Pentecostal church, or the A.M.E. church. Jesus Christ is our righteousness.

III. In verse 4, Paul points out that the purpose of the law is fulfilled in Christ, as the means of righteousness (that is right relationship to God) for everyone that trust in Him the law was just a schoolmaster until Christ came.

Now the believer in Christ has had imparted to him all the righteousness of God which is in Christ. Romans 3:21 says, "But now the righteousness of God without the law is manifested, being witnessed by the law and the prophets: even the righteousness of God which is by faith of Jesus Christ unto all and upon them that believe: for there is no difference".

A. Righteousness has been put to our account, when we came to Jesus, all of our past sins were done away with (forgiven) His death has taken care of our sins.
B. Keep in mind the problems with the Jews. (1) They were ignorant of God's righteousness. (2) They had gone about to establish their own righteousness. They were working to be accepted before God.

Paul is trying to get them understand that salvation is on an individual basis and that it is by faith. According to verse 8, the word of faith had been preached in contrast to the law.

IV. In Romans 10:9, there are three elements that are essential for salvation. Let's read before we close. "That if thou shalt confess with thy mouth the Lord Jesus, and shalt believe in thine heart that God hath raised Him from the dead, thou shalt be saved." The three elements are: believe, confess, and call.

A. Believe. It must be in the heart, not just a mind agreement. There must be a conviction in the heart, a firm persuasion in the heart. Notice in verse 9, that believing has to do especially with the resurrection of Christ. It is not merely believing that He died for our sins but also that, "God had raised Him from the dead." We believe also that He gives spiritual life to those who trust Him as Savior. Romans 5:10 says, "For if, when we were enemies, we were reconciled to God by the death of His Son, much more, being reconciled, we shall be saved by His life.

B. The second element is verse 9: confess. That if thou shalt confess with thy mouth the Lord Jesus. This is how we identify ourselves with Jesus Christ. We reveal to others that we belong to Him. Confess here means to speak the same thing, to agree with, it is a confession that Jesus Christ is Lord. This implies that He is God. A.T. Robertson said no Jew would call Jesus Lord, who had not really trusted Him. Confession with the mouth without believing in the heart is hypocrisy. On the other hand, believing in the heart without confession is cowardice. Confession is evidence to other that you believe in Jesus Christ as your personal Savior.

C. The third element is the "call". Romans 10:13 states a simple condition: "For whosoever shall call on the name of the Lord shall be saved." Salvation is a provision, but it is also provisional. That is it has been provided, but it must be appropriated." The provision is history. It stands as a fact. Appropriation depends on individual response.

The provision was made by an act of God, on hill called Calvary. Not by the fact that your grandfather was in the church, it's not by what your daddy gave to the church. Some of us would like to think that we have made our own provision, we will tell you in a snap. I've been singing in this choir for twenty five years, as though one's efforts produces salvation. God has done for us, what we could not do for ourselves.

Grandma said, "He made a way out of no way." The song writer said, "He's bridge over troubled water." But He gave His Son into the hands of sinful for men, He died on a cross one Friday, and was raised early Sunday morning.

Good News on Sunday Morning, 64

Notes:

David's Faith

Psalms 27

Faith is like salvation. It is personal. Your faith depends on you. How much do you trust the Lord? On a scale of one to ten, how would you rate your faith? Think about it for a moment? If you have decided to give yourself a five, you are in serious trouble. Because you don't have very much faith in the Lord, your faith is very weak. On a scale of one to ten, every born again believer ought to be able to say I'm a ten. David was a ten, and I can tell. It's right there in verse one, as a matter of fact the first three words of verse one tells me that David is a ten.

He says, "The Lord is." Think about that for a moment, "The Lord is." The Lord is (blank), all David had to do was to fill in the blank with his needs. Evidently David walked around with a check book on heaven's eternal bank, and he had been making deposit into the faith account. When David had a need, he just pull out his check book, and wrote in what he needed right behind where it said, "The Lord is." He just filled in the blank, right on the other side of "the Lord is."

Here's where we can emulate David, we need more Christians today who will declare "The Lord is." Notice David put the Lord first in this Psalms, if you want something from Him; you must make Him first in your life. He's first in the morning. He's first when things are well in your life. He's first when we pray, and if we make Him first when things are well with us, if we make Him first when we pray, then we will discover He won't be hard to talk with when we get in trouble.

I. Listen, to David, "The Lord is my light" evidently David knew something about the shadows and dark places. Perhaps it was when he was on the run from either king Saul or his son Absalom, he had to wander from time to time in the night. The flicker of a torch would reveal his location, and he had to depend on the Lord to guide his footsteps. Somebody here knows what I am talking about, you are living in darkness right now, and you don't know what your next step is going to be like. You don't know if you are going to fall off a cliff or step on some poisonous serpent. I know you are wearing a new suit, and you got a little money in your pocket and there is a smile on your face. But if the truth was known, it's dark in your life. You need David's kind of faith; you need David's check book. Then you can say with him, "The Lord is…. my light."

Is there anybody here ever needed some "light"? Have your troubles ever been so great, that even at noon day they blocked the glow of the sun. It's noon day, but it's midnight in your life. Join the psalmist, "The Lord is my light." David didn't have to guess, he didn't have to take chances in darkness. The Lord will turn on His light when I'm in darkness. My brothers and sister, if you live long enough, sooner or later darkness will cast her garment about you. Darkness may come in the form of a runaway daughter; your darkness may be drug infested son. Somebody's darkness might be their failing health.

You need David's faith; you need David's check book. "The Lord is my light." Job 29:3 says, "And when by His light I walked through darkness." I tell you in your darkest hour, The Lord is able to send Light, and the light He sends does not burn out. I John 1:5 declares that." God is light, and in Him there is no darkness. Now I know why grandmother use to sing "shine one me let it shine on me, let the light from the light house, shine on me." I tell you this is a dark world, if you are not able to say, "The Lord is my light."

Jesus said in John 8:12, "I am the light of the world he that followeth me shall not walk in darkness, but shall have the light of life." Don't fool yourself, you need light. Light is knowledge. It's revealing. Light is penetrating, and it stamps out darkness. Light is life, and nobody wants to live in darkness.

II. David shows out with his faith, not only is "the Lord my light," yes, yes, yes "the Lord is my salvation; whom shall I fear." There is spiritual salvation, and there is physical salvation. David is concerned here with the physical. The Lord is my (*Yesha*) my safety, in Greek it is pronounced (σωTnp) ((σωTnpia) my safety. This verse can be read, "The Lord is my light and my Savior."

He delivers me when danger comes. David is saying no matter what the danger is and no matter who brings the threat, "the Lord is my salvation." The Lord will deliver me. The Lord will make me safe. This kind of faith takes the worry out of life, and we do need something to take our problems away. One writer said, "Faith is acting like a thing is so when it isn't so in order that it might be so." Romans 8:31 says, "If God be for us, who can be against us." What can man do against a child of God? Satan cannot harm a child of God without God's permission.

The Lord is my safety. He is my deliverer. "The Lord is my salvation whom shall fear?" "Whom shall I fear?" I was riding down the freeway the other day and there was a car in front of me, and there was a sign in the rear window that said, "No fear." I thought about that sign and I said to myself that he's foolish, crazy, or too young to know any better.

Without the Lord, there are countless things that I fear. David is saying, "The Lord is my safety. No fear." I wonder do we have any fearless Christians here this morning. One day Saul in a jealous rage threw his spear at David, and the Lord moved David just in the nick of time. David had experienced the safety of the Lord. "No fear," this same David faced the giant Goliath with five smooth stones while the army of Israel shook in their boots. You can't say, "The Lord is my salvation," unless you have experience His deliverance. You can't say it, unless you have experienced His power to preserve you.

III. Listen! "The Lord is the strength of my life; of whom shall I be afraid." That word strength means stronghold, a strong fortified place. Not only is the Lord my safety, but He's my stronghold. He's a place where I can hide. No danger can reach me; nothing can take me from my stronghold. "The Lord is the strength of my life." He holds me together when I ought to be falling apart. He holds me together when I ought to be crumbling.

The world looks at me and wonders how he can keep going. When it's really not me, "The Lord is the strength of my life. Whom shall I fear?" David knew that faith and fear won't stay in the same body. To fear is to doubt the Lord, to trust is to have no fear.

It is said that fear knocked at the door, faith opened the door and no one was there. Faith and fear don't hang out together. Wherever faith is, fear is on the other side of town.

In Psalms 56:11, David said, "In God have I put my trust, I will not be afraid what man can do unto me." "I will not be afraid what man can do unto me." No fear. Proverbs 3:5 says, "Trust in the Lord with all thine heart; and lean not unto thine own understanding. In all thy ways acknowledge Him and He shall direct they path." There is no room for fear.

IV. Verse 2, I'm closing. When the wicked even mine enemies and my foes, came upon me to eat up my flesh, they stumbled and fell. An enemy is someone that use to be your friend. You know ya'll went to church together and ate Kentucky Fried Chicken out of the same bucket. Ya'll played cards together on Saturday nights. You even shared your secrets. But something went wrong and your friend became your enemy. Now a foe doesn't have to know you. They are willing to join your enemies in order to bring you down. A foe just likes mess. David said they came to destroy me, but "they stumbled and fell." I didn't see the hand that tripped them, but they stumbled and fell. I know it was the Lord who was on my side. That's why David said the Lord is my salvation every time his enemies thought they had him. They stumbled and fell. I didn't have to fight. I didn't have to curse, and I didn't have to argue. "They stumbled and fell."

"Though an host should encamp against me, my heart shall not fear: though war should rise against me in this will I be confident." In this will I trust. I trust in the Lord, not my own strength, not my speed, not my solider, not my money. "I trust in the Lord." He's my light. "He's a lamp unto my feet, and a light unto my path way." He lights my way in darkness. He's my deliverer. He's my hiding place. He's bread in a starving land. He's water in dry places. He's a friend when you are friendless. He's a mother, father, sister; he is a brother. I don't know what He is to you, but he is all I need.

One Friday evening He took my place on a hill call Calvary. He died on a cross. He was buried in a borrowed tomb. God raised Him early Sunday morning with all power in his hands. He's all I need.

Saved From What?

Ephesians 2:8

Saved from the penalty of sin. Genesis 2:17,"For in the day thou eatest thereof thou shalt surely die," Adam and Eve died spiritually and began dying physically when they disobeyed God in the garden of Eden, Spiritually they were separated from God. Physically their bodies began to age and die. Romans 5:12, "Wherefore, as by one man sin entered into the world, and death by sin; and so death passed upon all men for that all have sinned." The first sin brought ruin to the human race. "Sin entered into the world," and death followed, "death passed upon all men."

Adam's sin was imputed to his posterity, every human being was in the lions of Adam when he transgressed, according to Romans 5:12-14. Adam could only produce a likeness of himself, a sinful generation. The penalties on the sons and daughters of Adam are: (1) physical death, (2) spiritual death, and (3) the second death. Revelation 20:6, "Blessed and holy is he that hath part in the first resurrection: on such the second death has no power; but they shall be Priests of God and of Christ, and shall reign with Him a thousand years." Revelation 20:14, "And death and hell were cast into the lake of fire. This is the second death." This is eternal separation of the soul from God and banishment from His presence forever.

The penalty for sin is great, but it is not greater than that Grace that saves. God has not left us without hope. Romans 3:23, "For all have sinned, and come short of the glory of God." "All" is inclusive, it leaves no one out, Jews and Gentiles, have missed the mark, they have fail to keep the law. Romans 6:23, "For the wages of sin is death: but the gift of God is eternal life." Thank God for Grace.

Saved from what? Saved from the power of sin. Galatians 5:17, "For the flesh lusteth against the Spirit and the Spirit against the flesh: and these are contrary the one to the other: so that ye cannot do the things that ye would." In the believer there are two natures: the old nature and the new nature. The old nature is sometime referred to as sin, or the flesh. The old nature is what Adam passed on to us and it is sinful. And there is the new nature, which we receive at conversion, and the new nature is of divine origin, it is from above, it is a work of the Spirit. The old nature and the new nature never agree, there is a struggle between the two.

The only way that a Christian can have victory over the old nature is to apply Romans 5:16,"Walk in the Spirit and ye shall not fulfill the lust of the flesh." Verse 18, is very clear, "Be led of the Spirit," there is a need to be Spirit controlled. Ephesians 5:18, "Be filled with the Spirit." Saved from the power of sin is a work of the Holy Spirit on behalf of the believer. I John 3:9, "Whosoever is born of God doth not commit sin; for His seed remaineth in him: and he cannot sin, because he is born of God." The child of God does not have the habit of sin, "His Seed, the divine principle of life," is in him and he cannot go on sinning.

The power of sin has no control over a Spirit filled believer. If a person is filled with the Spirit there is no room for anything else. There are people in this modern age, claim spirituality, but their life style says differently. The Spirit is at work in their lives, from 11:00 A.M. on Sunday until 1:00 P.M., they act as though He is a part time Worker. The truth is, that He is at work twenty four seven. Ephesians 4:30, "And grieve not the Holy Spirit of God, whereby ye are sealed unto the day of redemption." When a Christian fails to tell the truth, it grieves the Holy Spirit, when a Christian entertains dirty thoughts, it grieves the Holy Spirit. The Spirit cannot work in your life when He is grieved; the fellowship with Him has been broken. Spirit controlled, or being Spirit led must be continuous, not intermittent.

It is impossible to speak of being saved from the power of sin, and not mentions Satan the tempter, he tempts humankind in three ways, the pride of life, the lust of the flesh, and the lust of the eye. In Genesis chapter three Eve was seduced on all three accounts, verse 6, "And when the woman saw that the tree was good for food," (the lust of the flesh), "And that it was pleasant to the eyes," (the lust of the eyes), "And a tree to be desired to make one wise" (the pride of life). In Matthew chapter four Jesus defeated Satan's attack with scripture, the word of God and the Holy Spirit is our best defense.

Saved from what? We shall be saved from the presence of sin. John 14:2-3, Jesus says, "In my Father's house are many mansions: if it were not so, I would have told you. I go to prepare a place for you. And if I go and prepare a place for you, I will come again, and receive you unto myself, that where I am, there ye may be also." "In my Father's house" is out of the presence of sin; it is a prepared place for those that accept Jesus Christ as their Lord and Savior.

In this world sin is everywhere, on your job, it comes into your home by way of television and radio, sin is in the shopping malls, men holding hands with men, women with women, the fear of a child being snatched and molested. Liquor stores on every corner, drugs are sold in our neighborhoods often by children. We shall be saved from the presence of sin, I

Thessalonians 4: 16, 17, "For the Lord Himself shall descend from heaven with the voice of the archangel, with the trump of God: and the dead in Christ shall rise first: then we which are alive and remain shall be caught up together with them in the clouds, to meet the Lord in the air: and so shall we ever be with the Lord." A perpetual residence with the Lord, a meeting without a parting, saved, delivered from the presence of sin. Hallelujah to the Lamb.

What is this Grace that saves? Merrill F. Unger wrote that, "Grace is what God may be free to do, and indeed what He does, accordingly, for the lost after Christ has died on behalf of them," and Unger is quoting Lewis Sperry Chafer. Then we must understand that Grace is unmerited, we did not do anything to deserve it, and certainly we cannot do anything to earn this Grace. Ephesians 2:9, "Not of works, lest any man should boast." We should work because God has saved us, never to be saved or to remain saved. Not only is Grace unmerited, but it is unmotivated as well, mankind was unattractive, stain by sin. Romans 5:8, "But God commendeth His love toward us, in that, while we were yet sinners, Christ died for us." Sin had brought ruin upon humankind; it had separated us from God.

Whatever God has done for us, it was without

merit, without influence from us. We were away from God, we had no strength to return, and we were without knowledge of how to return. We were taught at the Southern Bible Institute, that Grace is the unmerited favor of God; it is something that God gives that we don't deserve. L.V. Alexander's definition of Grace; "Grace is one of the many identities of God, He identifies Himself in Grace, which He is freely giving, and He reveals His purpose for the lost, and that is to save them from eternal damnation, even though we are unworthy."

Paul takes the word Grace, and it's definition or its meaning to express a fundamental characteristic of Christianity. Romans 11:5-6, "Even so then at this present time also there is a remnant according to the election of Grace. And if by Grace, then is no more of works: otherwise Grace is no more Grace." The International Standard Bible Encyclopedia defines Grace, in this sense is an attitude on God's part that proceeds entirely from within Himself, and that is conditioned in no way by anything in the objects of His favor. Perhaps there will be an even clearer definition of Grace, when we see our Savior face to face.

God has much more Grace than man will ever need, His Grace cannot be measured, or weighted.

God's Grace cannot be calculated, it cannot be computed, God will never run short on Grace. Charles H. Spurgeon wrote "A man is not rich when he can count his money, or miss this and that when he has spent it. When a person becomes immensely wealthy, he is richer than he needs to be, and has not only enough, but much more to spare. So is it with the Grace of God: He has as much Grace as you want, and He has a great deal more than that. God has as much Grace as the whole universe will require, but He has vastly more." Thanks be unto God for His Grace.

There is that Grace that saves, and there is what I call daily grace. God's Grace extends beyond the new birth; it is involved in our daily walk. In II Corinthians 12, the Apostle Paul speaks of a thorn in his flesh that was given to him, to keep him from being exalted above measure. In verse 8, Paul said, "For this I besought the Lord thrice, that it might depart from me." And the Lord answered him, "My grace is sufficient for thee: for my strength is made perfect in weakness." Is this not daily grace? John Newton wrote the hymn I love to sing; he must have known something of saving grace as well as daily grace.

Amazing grace! how sweet the sound,
That saved a wretch like me!
I once was lost but now am found,
Was blind but now I see.

'Twas grace that taught my heart to fear,
And grace my fears relieved;
How precious did that grace appear
The hour I first believed!

Thru many dangers, toils and snares
I have already come;
'Tis grace hath brought me safe thus far,
And grace will lead me home.

We may never understand grace totally in this life, but I am sure in the world to come all will be revealed. Perhaps I Corinthians 13:12, will explain, "For now we see through a glass, darkly; but then face to face; now I know in part; but then shall I know even as also I am known."

James M. Boice, wrote in his book The Doctrine of Grace, "God allows the goodness of creation to shine even in places where the Lordship of Jesus Christ is not yet acknowledged, this goodness is the product of His common grace, by which He maintains human existence, relaxes His curse against sin, arrests the process of decay, and thus allows human culture to develop." I don't like the phrase, that God relaxes His curse against sin. But my concern is common grace; it must be the expression of God to human kind. Matthew 5:45, "For He maketh the sun to rise on the evil and the good, and sendeth rain on the just and on the unjust."

Thanks be unto God for his saving grace, His daily grace, and for His common grace. "For by Grace are ye saved through faith," am I hearing Paul correctly? Because what I am hearing is that faith must be present before grace can save. Faith must be demonstrated, acted upon, or acted out before grace can save. Receiving saving grace is predicated upon ones faith. If this is true then we must find a working definition of faith. Biblical faith, or Christian faith, is belief and trust in God.

Unger wrote, "The word faith is used in scripture, (1) Most frequently in a subjective sense, denoting a moral and spiritual quality of individuals, by virtue of which men are held in relations of confidence in God and fidelity to Him. (2) In an objective sense, meaning the body of truth, moral and religious, which God has revealed - that which men believe."

Faith is to be practiced; it is to be lived out daily. While it reveals truth, it is faith that binds man to that truth, wherein it is not burdensome, but joyful. Faith is properly defined as the conviction of the reality of the truths and facts, which God has revealed, such conviction resting solely upon the testimony of God. I have discovered that faith cannot be totally explained, it cannot be totally defined, it must be experienced, it must be practiced, and it must be tested. If it were so that we express our faith in order to acquire salvation, then faith must be practiced daily, that we might walk by faith and not by sight.

We must never forget that faith is the condition of salvation. It is not the procuring cause, but the condition, or the instrumental cause. Romans 10:17, "So then faith cometh by hearing, and hearing by the word of God." Paul seems to suggest that we had no faith, we were poverty-stricken, and it was the word of God that impregnated us with faith. We had nothing, but sin and guilt. In order to be save it is absolutely necessary to hear the word of God. Let me just mention that the word of God will reveal our sin and offer a cure, the word reveals judgment for sin and give a way of escape.

The death, burial, and resurrection of Jesus Christ is the central theme of the word of God.

Hebrews 4:12, "For the word of God is quick; and powerful, and sharper than any twoedged sword, piercing even to the dividing asunder of soul and spirit, and of the joints and marrow, and is a discerner of the thoughts and intents of the heart." The word of God is living, effective, and self-fulfilling, it diagnoses the condition of the human heart, saying, "Thou ailest here, and there," it brings blessing to those who receive it in faith and pronounce judgment on those who disregard it. I Peter 1:23, "Being born again, not of corruptible seed, but of incorruptible, by the word of God, which liveth and abideth forever."

A clear description of the word of God by Peter is "The word of God liveth and abideth forever." This word is powerful enough to deposit faith in a sinner. The word of God breeds faith with the saved and the unsaved. Isaiah 55:11, "So shall my word be that goeth forth out of my mouth it shall not return unto me void, but it shall accomplish that which I please, and it shall prosper in the thing whereto I sent it."

Faith runs like a silver cord through the Bible, from Genesis to Revelation. Hebrews 11:1-2, "Now faith is the substance of things hoped for, the evidence of things not seen. For by it the elders obtained a good report." That is to say, things, which in themselves have no existence yet, become real and substantial by the exercise of faith. There are two note-worthy words I would like to mention here, "conviction" and "assurance." Hebrews 11:6, "But without faith it is impossible to please God: for he that cometh to God must believe that He is, and that He is a rewarder of them that diligently seek Him."

If man is going to do business with God, that business will be predicated on faith alone, there is no other way. It is said that Abraham was a friend of God, was it because he believed God? Noah believed God, and his whole house was saved from the flood, that is all that God requires, trust me, trust me, trust me. Psalms 125:1, "They that trust in the Lord shall be as mount Zion, which cannot be removed, but abideth for ever." The secret to consistency is to trust in God because He never changes, people change, religions change with time, new ideas, new leaders. But God remain the same, He is completely reliable and will keep us steady, physically, and spiritually.

According to Ephesians 2:9 Paul says, "And that not of yourselves: it is the gift of God: not of works, lest any man should boast." There is nothing man can do to earn salvation, and certainly there is nothing that can be done, humanly speaking. Notice the parallelism between verse 8, and verse 9, (not your own doing…not because of works). The qualifying clauses are simply emphasizing salvation by grace.

It needs to be understood that salvation is a work of God on man's behalf, it is not a work of God on man's behalf with man's help. We have no strength, no power to help ourselves; God alone provides our provisions. No life has been good enough for God, except that of His only begotten Son, Romans 3:23, "For all have sinned and come short of the glory of God." "All" leaves no man; woman, boy, or girl out.

Theodore H. Epp wrote in his book, How God Makes Bad Men Good, there are three basic aspects of sin. First sin is an act. It is a violation of or a lack of obedience to God's known will. This is the aspect of sin that is commonly thought of when the word sin is mentioned, but there are more aspects than this. Secondly sin is a state, sin is the absence of righteousness, and in this sense it is more than an act; it is a state of being.

Thirdly, sin is also a nature, Paul mention the sin nature in Romans 7:15-21, he said that there is a struggle between the old nature (sin nature) and the new nature. I'm always doing what I don't want to do;

I want to do good, but how to perform that which is good I find not. Every person has a sin nature inherited from Adam, and because of this all are condemned, regardless of the extent to which individuals express their sin nature. Man could do nothing for himself, sin was too powerful for him, and the muscles, the forcefulness, and the attraction of sin prove to be too much for him, that's where grace is applied.

"And that not of yourselves: it is the gift of God: not of works, lest any man should boast." Paul wants humankind to know that you have no part in salvation; it is a work of God on man's behalf. "For all have sinned, and come short of the glory of God." We could not help ourselves, we were a condemned race. We have nothing to boast of, we were poverty stricken. God's grace alone has saved us, thanks be unto God for His saving grace.

Good News on Sunday Morning, 88

Notes:

A Miniature Bible

John 3:16

St. John 3:16, is a miniature Bible in itself, it encompass time from Genesis to Revelation, it leaves no one out. This scripture speaks to Jews and Gentiles; it gives us a mental picture of God the Father, God the Son, and God the Holy Spirit. Its content is informative enough to save sinners, and powerful enough to transform the worst of us. God's love is on display, it motivated Him to give all He had to save lost sinners.

The English language cannot define God's love, our words fail, and they fall short. God's love is best defined by His gift, "His only begotten Son." His love for the lost is best understood in His gift. Love is an action word, God is always giving, James 1:17, "Every good gift and every perfect is from above, and cometh down from the Father of lights, with whom is no variableness, neither shadow of turning." John 3:16, is one of many scriptures that informs us that salvation is by faith in Jesus Christ, nothing more, and certainly nothing less. St. John 3:16, "For God so loved the world, that He gave His only begotten Son, that whosoever believeth in Him should not perish, but have everlasting life."

God who is the Creator and Sustainer of the universe puts His love on display for lost sinners to see, that He is not so distance in His Holiness that He is not concern about man. Although He hates sin, He cannot look on sin, yet His love shines forth toward sinners. It is a humbling experience to know that God who is all-powerful and all wise has made provisions for sinners.

Romans 5:6-8, points out our helplessness, and God's love on our behalf, "For when were yet without strength, in due time Christ died for the ungodly. For scarcely for righteous man will one die: yet peradventure for a good man some would even dare to die. But God commendeth His love toward us, in that, while we were yet sinners, Christ died for us." While we were aliens, unfriendly, lawless, while we were filthy, and low down. While we were unable to respond to His love, God expressed His love toward us, He gave His only begotten Son to die for our sins.

It is clear that agape is divine love, the highest form of love, yet we struggle when we attempt to define God's love. The human language is inadequate, it falls short. The best definition of God's love can be understood in His gift, He gave His best, and He gave His all for lost sinners. "He gave His only begotten Son, that whosoever believeth in Him should not perish, but have everlasting life." God's love is without prejudice, "All have sinned and come short of the glory of God."

Whatever it takes to save the rich man, it is the same for the poor man, Ephesians 2:8, "For by grace are ye saved through faith; and that not of yourselves: it is the gift of God." It is faith in Jesus Christ that saves, I would like to think that grace is a product of God's love; His grace meets the needs of the lost. Lewis Sperry Chafer says, "Grace is what God may be free to do, and indeed what He does, accordingly, for the lost after Christ has died on their behalf." Unger's says, "That grace rules out human merit."

"For God so loved the world, that He gave His only begotten Son, that whosoever believeth in Him should not perish, but have everlasting life." God gave His Son to us and He gave Him for us, He gave Him to us at Bethlehem and He gave Him for us at Calvary. The babe in the manger, born of a virgin, without romantic involvement, what a marvelous sight, the Christ child is born in Bethlehem. Matthew 1:21, "And she shall bring forth a Son, and thou shall call His name Jesus: for He shall save His people from their sins." Verse 23, "Behold a virgin shall be with child, and shall bring forth a Son, and they shall call His name Emmanuel, which being interpreted is, God with us."

If it were true that God is with us, in the

person of the babe in Bethlehem, we can be sure that He has come to do us good. He identifies with us in the likeness of human flesh. He was to teach us how to utter the words, "Our Father," we could never conceive this on our own, we had drifted to far from God. Sin had separated us from our Creator, and we could not find our way back to God. Emmanuel came to planet earth to show us the Father, in John 14:8, Philip makes an unusual request, "Lord show us the Father, and it sufficeth us. Jesus said unto him, have I been so long time with you, and yet hast thou not known me, Philip? He that hath seen Me hath seen the Father; and how sayest thou then, show us the Father?"

At Calvary, God gave His Son for us, He took the sinners place on a Roman cross, hung, bled, and died He was our substitute. He was without sin, yet He died for sinners, the Just dying for the unjust, Matthew 1:21b, "for He shall save His people from their sins." Christ death was a necessary penalty, which He bore for the sinner. Romans 4:25, "Who was delivered for our offences, and was raised for our justification." God gave His Son for us at Calvary, thank God for Jesus Christ.

"For God so loved the world, that He gave His only begotten Son, that whosoever believeth in Him should not perish, but have everlasting life." Whosoever is a wide word, it leaves no one out Jews and Gentiles, the learned and the unlearned, the good, the bad, and the ugly. Paul makes use of this wide word in Romans 10:11, "For the scripture saith, Whosoever believeth on Him shall not be ashamed." Again in verse 13, "For whosoever shall call upon the name of the Lord shall be saved." This word should bring joy to every sinner's heart; it informs us that God has made provisions for all through His Son. "Whosoever" means, whatever person, any person.

"For God so loved the world, that He gave His only begotten Son, that whosoever believeth in Him should not perish, but have everlasting life." "Whosoever," (any person, whatever person) "believeth in Him should no perish, but have everlasting life." It is faith in Jesus Christ, the Son of God that saves, nothing needs to be added. Ephesians 2:8, "For by grace are ye saved through faith; and that not of yourselves: it is the gift of God:" Verse 9, "Not of works, lest any man should boast."

Anything added to faith in order to be saved is works and a misuse of Scripture. A simple definition of faith, biblical faith is belief, it is trust in God. Faith is defined as the conviction of the reality of the truths and facts, which God has revealed, such conviction resting solely upon the testimony of God. When we believe in Jesus Christ, we practice His precepts, He is our lawgiver, and He sets the standards. We trust Christ now and we trust Him for eternity.

What must a sinner believe? That Jesus is the Christ, the Son of the living God, born of a virgin, died on the cross for our sins, and was raised on that third day morning for our justification. John 20:30-31,"And many other signs truly did Jesus in the presence of His disciples, which are not written in this book. However, these are written, that ye might believe that Jesus is the Christ, the Son of God; and that believing ye might have life through His name. Jonah 2:9,"Salvation is of the Lord."

Notice John 3:16, "Believe in Jesus Christ," that is to have confidence in Him, trust Him, rely on Him, for life eternal. This is more than intellectual faith, it is more than emotions. I believe that when faith is activated or applied, intellectual faith and emotions becomes a reality. When faith is genuine, there must be some degree of intellect to believe, some emotion because of appreciation, for what the Lord has done. Intellect will hear information, collect data, and make a decision.

Emotion is a human reaction for what the

Lord has done; it has much to do with feelings. Believing in Jesus Christ becomes a matter of the heart, when the heart is changed the life is new, Proverbs 4:23, "Keep thy heart with all diligence; for out of it are the issues of life." Jesus makes it clear in Matthew 15:18,"But those things which proceeds out the mouth comes forth from the heart; and they defile the man. For out of the heart proceed evil thoughts, murder adulteries, fornications thefts, false witness, and blasphemies." Psalms 51:10, David says, "Create in me a clean heart, O God; and renew a right spirit within me."

When the heart is changed, the life style will become Christ like,, Ezekiel 11:19-20, "And I will give them one heart, and I will put a new spirit within you; and I will take the stony heart out of their flesh, and will give them an heart of flesh: that they may walk in my statutes, and they shall be my people, and I will be their God." Heart trouble is what sinners are suffering with, and the only cure is Jesus Christ.

"For God so loved the world, that He gave His only begotten Son, that whosoever believeth in Him should not perish, but have everlasting life." "Should not perish" (*apoletai*), this does not mean annihilation but rather final destiny of ruin and doom in hell, eternal separation from God. "But have everlasting life," the gift of God, so precious is this gift eternal life, it is fellowship with God throughout eternity. John3:17, "For God sent not His Son into the world to condemn the world; but that the world through Him might be saved." Salvation is available through faith in Jesus Christ, sinners need only to accept this gift.

References

Holy Bible KJV, Edited by C.I. Scofield D.D.

Major Bible Themes, Lewis S. Chafer, Revised by John F. Walvoord

Unger's Bible Dictionary, Merrill F. Unger

The International Standard Bible Encyclopedia, Vol. II, James Orr, General Editor; Morris O. Evans, Managing Editor; Melvin Grove Kyle, Revising Editor

Tyndale New Testament Commentaries, Ephesians, Francis Foulkes

The New International Commentary on The New Testament, The Epistle of Hebrews, F.F. Bruce

Spurgeon's Expository Encyclopedia Vol. VIII, Charles H. Spurgeon

The Doctrines of Grace, James Montgomery Boice, Philip Graham Ryken

How God Makes Bad Men Good, Theodore H. Epp

www.ingramcontent.com/pod-product-compliance
Lightning Source LLC
Chambersburg PA
CBHW032147040426
42449CB00005B/423